DRAGONS AND WIZARDS
CD-ROM AND BOOK

MARTY NOBLE
AND
ERIC GOTTESMAN

DOVER PUBLICATIONS, INC.
MINEOLA, NEW YORK

Bibliographical Note

Dragons and Wizards CD-ROM and Book, published by Dover Publications, Inc., in 2003, contains all of the images shown in the book *Dragons: A Book of Designs* by Marty Noble, originally published by Dover Publications, Inc., in 2002, plus sixteen pages (pages 33-48) newly rendered by Marty Noble and Eric Gottesman.

Dover Electronic Clip Art®

International Standard Book Number: 0-486-99559-3

Manufactured in the United States of America
Dover Publications, Inc., 31 East 2nd Street, Mineola, N.Y. 11501

The CD-ROM on the inside back cover contains all of the images shown in the book. There is no installation necessary. Just insert the CD into your computer and call the images into your favorite software (refer to the documentation with your software for further instructions). Each image has been scanned at 600 dpi and saved in six different formats—BMP, EPS, GIF, JPEG, PICT, and TIFF. The JPEG and GIF files—the most popular graphics file types used on the Web—are Internet-ready.

The "Images" folder on the CD contains a number of different folders. All of the TIFF images have been placed in one folder, as have all of the PICT, all of the EPS, etc. The images in each of these folders are identical except for file format. Every image has a unique file name in the following format: xxx.xxx. The first 3 or 4 characters of the file name, before the period, correspond to the number printed with the image in the book. The last 3 characters of the file name, after the period, refer to the file format. So, 001.TIF would be the first file in the TIFF folder.

Also included on the CD-ROM is Dover Design Manager, a simple graphics editing program for Windows that will allow you to view, print, crop, and rotate the images.

For technical support, contact:
Telephone: 1 (617) 249-0245
Fax: 1 (617) 249-0245
Email: dover@artimaging.com
Internet: **http://www.dovertechsupport.com**
The fastest way to receive technical support is via email or the Internet.

1: France (12th century).   2 and 4: France (15th century).   3 and 5: Celtic.

4

6-9: Heraldry, Western Europe (14th–17th century).

10: Europe (16th century).   11 and 12: France (16th century).

13: France (16th century).   14: Germany (16th century).   15: Italy (17th century).   16. Germany (16th century).   17. Denmark.

18: Michael Maier, Prague (1617).   19: Germany (16th century).   20: Norman England.

21: European zodiac symbol.   22: England (17th century).

23: England (13th century).   24: Saturn, Babylonia.   25: Europe (17th century).
26: Herbrandt Jamsthaler, Germany (17th century).
27: India (19th century).

28: General.   29: England (late 19th century).   30: William Blake, England (19th century).
31: Michael Maier, Prague (1617).   32: Gustave Doré, France (19th century).

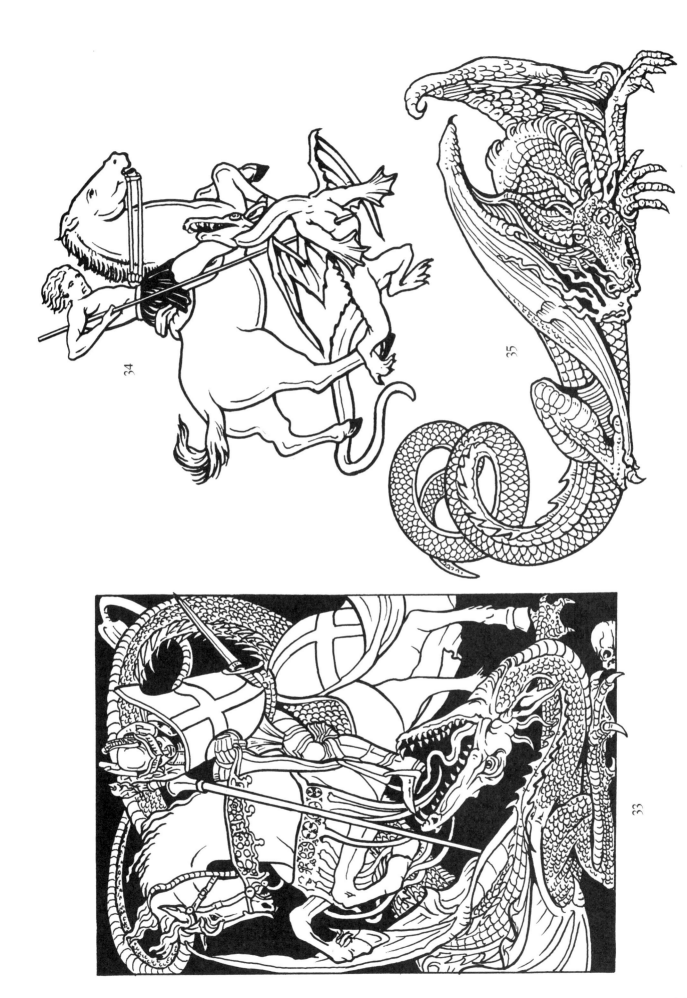

34

35

33

33 and 35: Walter Crane, England (1860s).   34: England (late 19th century).

11

36–40: General.

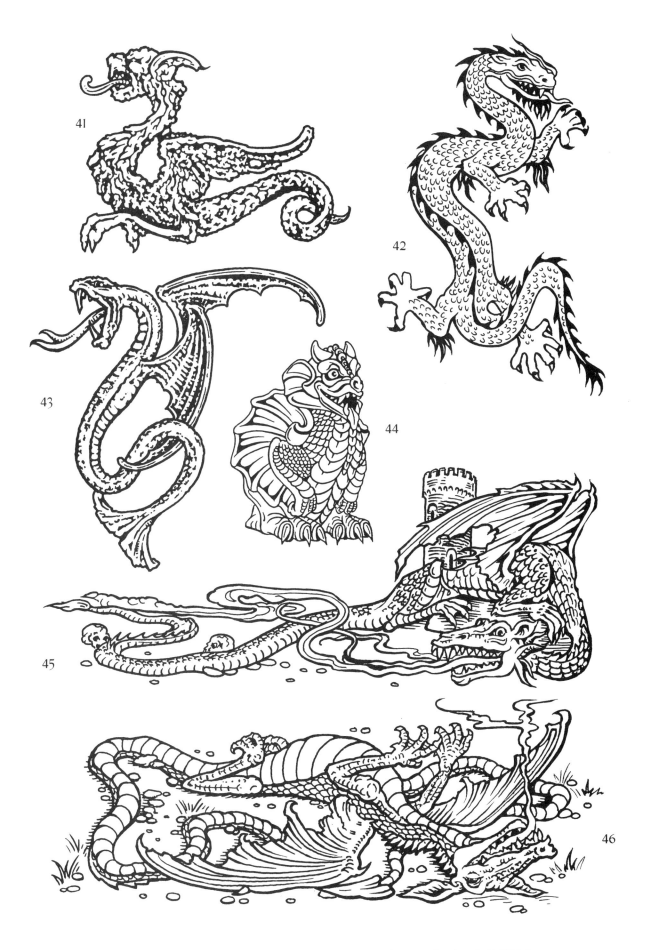

41–44: General.   45 and 46: Walter Crane, England (1860s).

13

47–50: General.   51. William Blake, England (19th century).

52–53: General.

54: Italy.   55: Europe (16th century).   56: Brescia, Italy (17th century).
57 and 58: Italy (16th century).

59

60

61

62

59–62: Japan.

63-67: Japan.

68 and 70: China.   69 and 71: Japan.

72: Greece.　　　73: Italy.　　　74 and 76: Java.　　　75: Indonesia.

77: Babylonia.   78, 80, and 82: Tibet.   79: Sikkim, India.   81: Indonesia.

21

83: Sufi, Middle East.   84: Bhutan, Himalayas.   85: Greece.   86: China.
87: Tibet.   88: Persia.

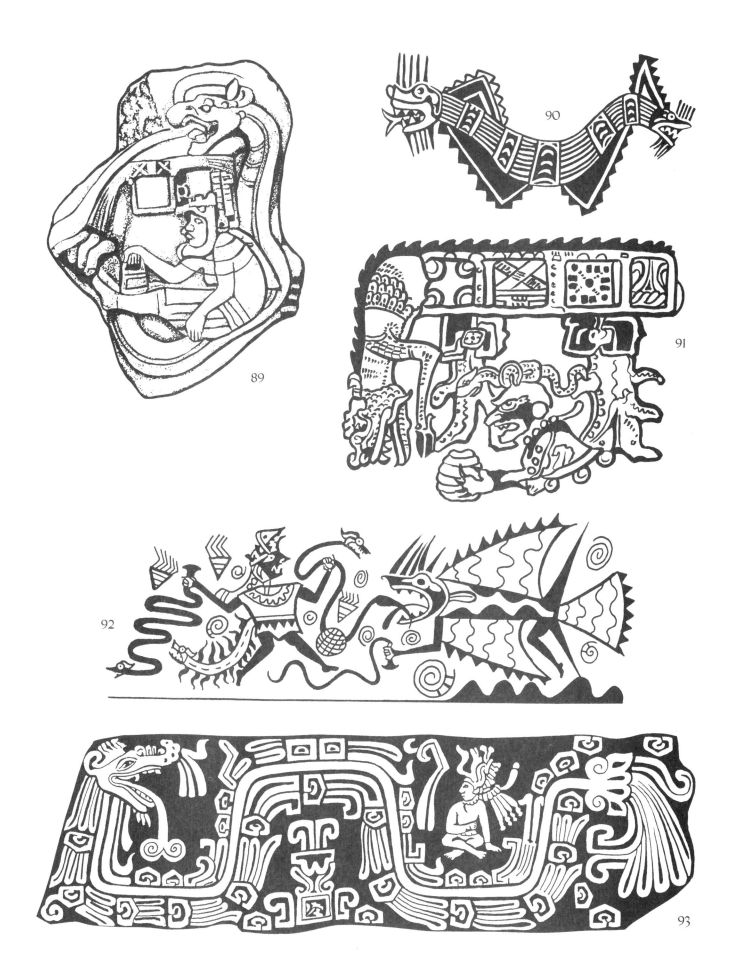

89: Olmec, ancient Mexico.   90: Peru.   91: Mayan civilization, ancient Mexico and
Central America.   92: Peru.   93: Xochicalco, ancient Mesoamerican site.

94

95

96

94 and 96: China.   95: Korea.

97

98

99

97–99: China.

100–104: China.

105–108: China.

109–111: China.

110

109

110

三

28

112–114: China.

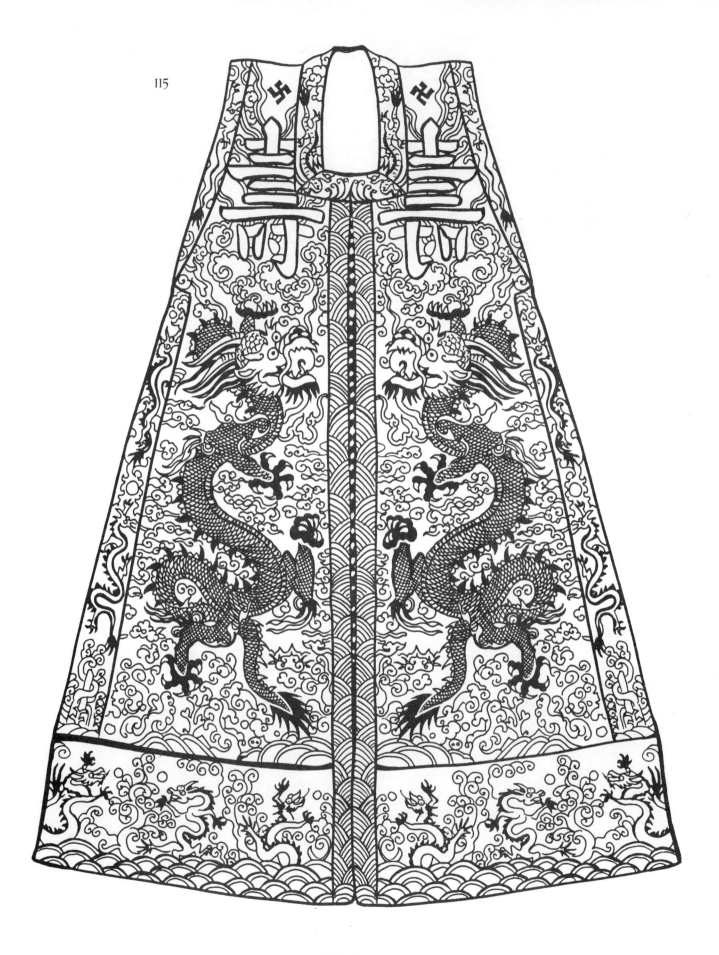

115: China.

115

116: China.

116

117

118

117–118: China.

121

124: Sorceress.

124

120

119, 120, and 123: Wizards.   121 and 122: Dragons.

123

119

122

125 and 128: Wizards.   126, 127, and 129: Dragons.   130: Wizard and Dragon.

131: Dragon.   132 and 133: Sorceresses.   134: Wizard and Dragon.

135 and 136: Dragons.   137: Sorcerer and Dragon.   138 and 139: Wizards.

140: Sorcerer.　　　141 and 143: Wizards.　　　142: Sorceress.

144

145

146

144–147: Sorcerers.

147

151

148

150

149

148, 149, and 151: Dragons.   150: Sorcerer and Dragon.

152: Dragon.   153: Wizard.   154: Sorceress and Dragon.

155: Wizard.   156: Dragon.   157: Sorcerer.   158 and 159: Sorceresses.

160 and 161: Wizards.   162: Sorcerer.   163: Sorceress.

164: Sorceress.   165 and 166: Wizards.   167: Sorcerer.

168   169

170   171

168, 169, and 170: Wizards.   171: Sorceress.

172 and 175: Sorceresses.   173: Wizard.   174: Dragon.

176 and 179: Wizards.   177 and 178: Sorceresses.

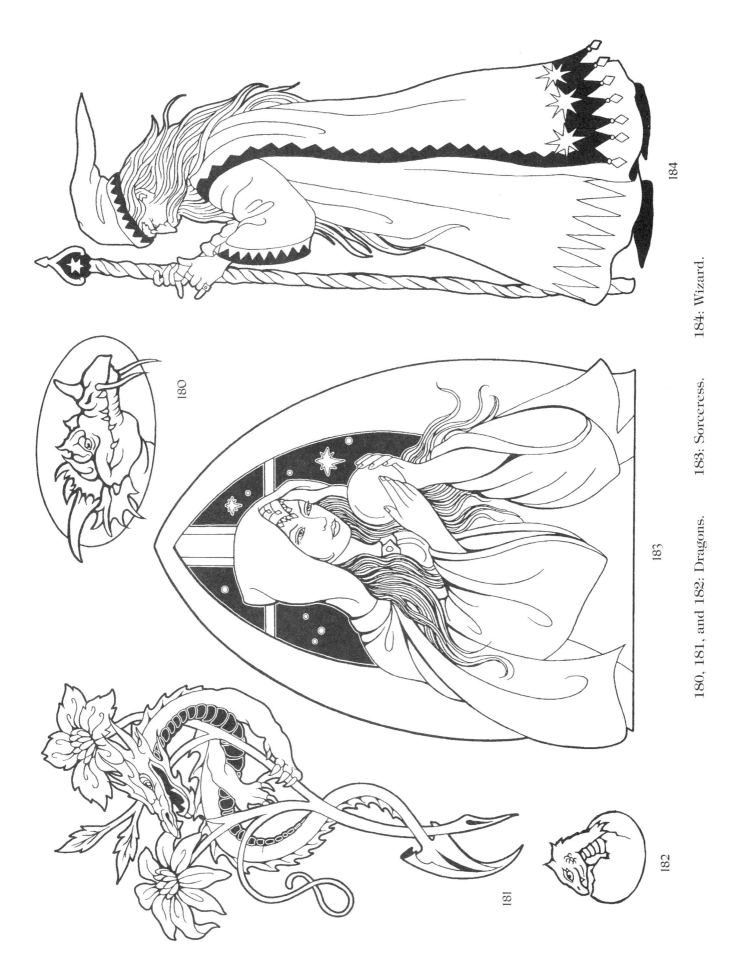

184: Wizard.   183: Sorceress.

180, 181, and 182: Dragons.

184

180

183

181

182

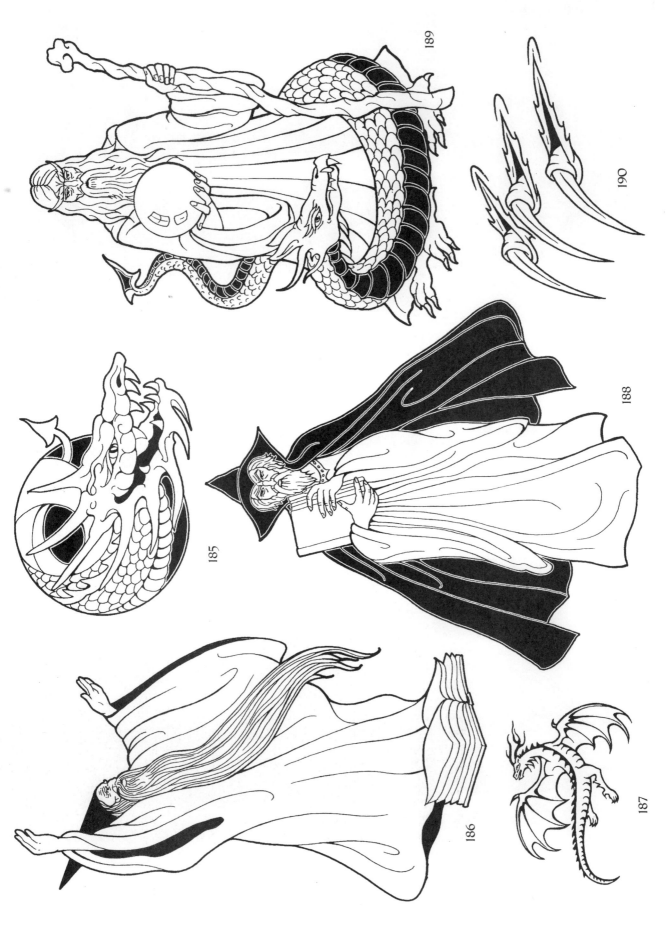

185, 187, and 190: Dragons.   186 and 188: Wizards.   189: Sorcerer and Dragon.